SOCRATES

THE FATHER OF ETHICS AND INQUIRY

SOCRATES
THE FATHER OF ETHICS
AND INQUIRY

NATASHA DHILLON & JUN LIM

ROSEN
PUBLISHING
NEW YORK

Published in 2016 by The Rosen Publishing Group, Inc.
29 East 21st Street, New York, NY 10010

Library of Congress Cataloging-in-Publication Data

Dhillon, Natasha C., author.
Socrates : the father of ethics and inquiry/Natasha C. Dhillon and Jun
Lim.—First Edition.
    pages cm.—(The greatest Greek philosophers)
Includes bibliographical references and index.
ISBN 978-1-4994-6134-3 (library bound)
1. Socrates—Juvenile literature. 2. Philosophers—Greece—Biography—
Juvenile literature. I. Lim, Jun, author. II. Title.
B316.D49 2015
183'.2—dc23

                                                              2014048440
Manufactured in the United States of America

CONTENTS

The fifth century BCE was a time of remarkable progress for the city-state of Athens. Its military triumphed over powerful adversaries; political leaders were witnessing the benefits of the world's first democracy; artists produced masterpieces of painting, sculpture, and architecture; and ordinary Athenians luxuriated in the city-state's recently acquired wealth. Amid this cultural abundance, one man—barefoot and clothed in an old robe—would nurture another kind of richness: that of the intellect. That man would be known as one of the greatest philosophers for millennia to come. His name was Socrates.

Today we understand philosophy to encompass some of the greatest and most eternal questions, many of which have existed since the dawn of human thought. However, it was only during this golden age of Athens that Western philosophy would begin to develop as a separate and concrete discipline. Indeed, the word *philosophy* itself is rooted in the Greek for "the love of wisdom."

Although Socrates was a controversial figure during his life, he is remembered today as one of the fathers of moral philosophy.

The cultural climate of ancient Athens was ripe for Socrates's teachings. With its increased wealth came increased leisure time. This meant that elite and ordinary citizens alike could devote time to intellectual pursuits and grand questions of ethics and existence. Heated discussions about science, truth, and morality would erupt in the crowded marketplaces of Athens, captivating, enlightening, and informally educating those who stopped to listen. Learning was no longer a luxury reserved for only the educated and leisure classes. The streets of Athens served as a breeding ground for the philosophical ideas that we would study and practice in modern times. This philosophical theater had its regular scholars, who walked around daily, refining their skills of argument, and ordinary bystanders, who would jump into these passionate discussions.

Socrates became the greatest embodiment of this philosophical spirit. He was a largely self-educated and self-trained thinker. He heckled passersby—young or old, commoner or elite—until they would agree to engage with him on questions of morality, truth, and virtue. Through these debates, Socrates inspired people to question their assumptions and examine their own moral characters. Debates and verbal discussions were the primary forms in which he communicated his principles. In fact, no known writings of his exist at all. But Socrates gained a large following of young, curious intellectuals—including Plato and Xenophon—who would go on to immortalize Socrates's teachings in writings and discussions of their own.

Socrates's core interest in morality and ethics—knowing what is right and acting accordingly—did not change over his lifetime, but unfortunately for him, Athens did. At the turn of the fourth century BCE, Athens saw its democracy suspended, many of its citizens killed by disease and war, and all sense of security destroyed. Even during his prime, Socrates was a controversial figure who was often ridiculed in notable comic plays. However, when Athens fell from its golden-age perch, the once progressive society that fostered and tolerated his outspoken views turned on Socrates. After facing trial for corrupting Athenian youth, rejecting the accepted gods, and worshipping other gods, he would be condemned and executed for his ideas.

Thanks in large part to the followers who remained by his side even when much of Athens did not, however, Socrates's ideas did not die with him. His teachings have gained new audiences—and new meaning—with each subsequent generation and remain relevant even today.

CHAPTER ONE

EARLY LIFE

If Socrates himself maintained any records of his life or teachings, those writings have long been lost to history. What we know about Socrates comes entirely from the works of his contemporaries and followers. It has been said that he believed writing was detrimental to thought because it does not allow individuals to exchange ideas as openly and quickly as they could in an oral debate. Additionally, he thought writing encouraged people to feel freer to forget information that they could later look up, which enabled them to learn only superficially. Whatever his reasoning for not writing anything down, it has long frustrated historians and scholars who, centuries after his death, continue to rummage for clues about his life. The few definite details about Socrates's life that scholars have discovered are culled from secondhand sources—most of which were written after Socrates's death—penned by just three men: Aristophanes, Plato, and Xenophon.

A CRITIC'S PERSPECTIVE

The earliest surviving writings on Socrates are attributed to the comic playwright Aristophanes (c. 448–385 BCE). In his play *The Clouds*, Aristophanes parodied Socrates and his disciples, portraying the old sage as the manager of an airy, insubstantial school whose students' heads were in the clouds as they discussed vague, lofty matters that bore little relation to daily reality down here on earth. Aristophanes used clouds as a metaphor for Socrates's contemplation of vague, fluffy ideas that floated far above the practical problems of life on the ground and in the streets. *The Clouds* doesn't shed much light on Socrates's life, but it does show that the philosopher, while still living, was prominent enough of a figure to be worthy of a popular playwright's mockery.

A DEDICATED PUPIL

Plato (c. 428–348 BCE), one of Socrates's disciples who later become a much-acclaimed philosopher in his own right, wrote dialogues (a sort of philosophical

Although Plato founded the Academy in Athens, which inspired the fresco The School of Athens *by Raphael, after Socrates's death, Socrates is depicted in the green robe, left of Plato (center left) and facing away, in this detail of the fresco.*

debate play), many of which featured Socrates as a central figure. In his early dialogues, Plato depicted his former teacher engaged in hypothetical (or imaginary) conversations with students, friends, and well-known Athenian leaders of the time. It is hard to determine whether these dialogues depict an authentic Socrates or whether they serve as a mouthpiece for Plato's own philosophical thoughts.

The uncertainty arises because Plato's dialogues were written after Socrates's death. Plato may have relied on his memory of Socrates's debates to record his teacher's thoughts in the dialogues. In addition, Plato had his own ambitions as a philosopher, and these may have colored his depiction of Socrates. Plato's early works, including *Apology* and *Crito*, are generally regarded as accurate showcases of Socrates's philosophies. Plato's later dialogues, however, are viewed as his own theories presented through the utterances of a Socrates treated more as a literary figure than a historical one.

A BIOGRAPHER'S MISSION

Though Plato's works are thought to provide the most reliable information about Socrates's life and thought, the dialogues of military general Xenophon (c. 433–355 BCE) are perhaps more useful in providing an understanding of Socrates's fate. A former disciple of Socrates's, Xenophon was the last contemporary biographer of Socrates whose works on the thinker have survived.

Xenophon's dialogues were released a few decades after the philosopher was sentenced to death. They were intended to preserve and defend the memory and wisdom of his former teacher against the people who continued to condemn Socrates long after his execution. *Memorabilia of Socrates* and *Apology* depict Socrates's trial and the last days of his life. There are suggestions that Xenophon may have written *Memorabilia* and *Apology* partly to ease the guilt he felt for his role in Socrates's condemnation. As will be seen later, when Socrates was on trial before the Athenian court, the close relationship between Xenophon and Socrates strongly influenced the ruling that would end the life of the general's much-respected master.

UPBRINGING AND STUDIES

Socrates was born around 470 BCE in a village on the slopes of Mount Lycabettus, which was about a twenty-minute walk to Athens. Today, Athens is the capital of Greece, but at that time it was a powerful and independent city-state, a small nation unto itself. Socrates was raised in a household that was considered to be neither wealthy nor poor. His father, Sophroniscus, worked with stone, either as a stonecutter or a sculptor. When Socrates was old enough, he learned the stoneworkers' trade under the tutelage of his father.

Mount Lycabettus, the birthplace of Socrates, can still be seen rising over the city of Athens, Greece.

Socrates's mother, Phaenarete, worked as a midwife (a woman who helps other women give birth). In ancient Greece, women worked outside the home only if their financial or marital circumstances made it necessary. Most of these women worked out of fear of poverty because they were either single or widowed and struggling to make ends meet. Sophroniscus's work probably helped support the family well enough, so it's unclear why Socrates's mother also held a job.

Socrates is thought to have received an elementary education typical among male Athenian youths at the time, including the study of music, literature, and gymnastics. He also received extensive instruction in geometry, astronomy, and natural science, which was uncommon. There is evidence that he was a pupil of fifth-century BCE philosopher Archelaus, who in turn studied under Anaxagoras (500–428 BCE), a Greek philosopher who was born in Asia Minor but moved to Athens. Anaxagoras was primarily concerned with cosmology and theories of motion and creation, including the origins and development of matter and living things.

Socrates's early interest in this kind of scientific inquiry eventually gave way in his adult life to an almost exclusive focus on moral and ethical inquiry—what is a good life, and how does one live it? Plato's and Xenophon's dialogues indicate that Socrates spent almost no time pondering matters related to physics or cosmology, apparently considering them unimportant to questions about human nature, moral development, and destiny.

HONORABLE SERVICE

Before he became a teacher, Socrates earned his keep as a stonecutter. On several occasions, he also served as a soldier in the Athenian army.

Though Athens enjoyed a peaceful period during Socrates's young adulthood and into his middle age, Athens did engage in a few minor military campaigns. Athens had a large civilian militia in which citizens were on call to fight if and when they were needed. After serving in battles, soldiers returned to civilian life.

Socrates was called to duty on at least two campaigns, the first when he was in his thirties, against the city-state

ETHICS

Ethics is a branch of philosophy that addresses what is right and wrong and how to live a moral life. For this reason, ethics is also called moral philosophy. It is now a branch of philosophy, but the questions it raises are applicable to nearly every other discipline and to everyday life. Socrates was one of the first ethical philosophers in the West. But Socrates never preached about what he personally believed to be morally right or wrong. He would challenge students and other debate partners on their moral beliefs. In the act of defending to him what they thought was correct, they would determine for themselves how they should approach moral thought and why their previous way of thinking was insufficient.

Socrates wanted to help people understand and practice virtue for themselves and toward others. However, he never suggested that he himself was virtuous or that he had a special knowledge of morality. Ethical concerns remained Socrates's primary interest for the rest of his life.

Like the figure depicted on this piece of pottery, Socrates was a hoplite in his youth. Hoplites had heavier armor than foot soldiers who came before and had many great successes in battle.

Samos, and the second, when he was nearly forty, in the battle against the city-state Potidaea. He fought as a hoplite, or a foot soldier. Hoplites had to supply their own armor, so people of the middle class were generally the only ones who were wealthy enough to be able to serve in this division. Socrates did not fight in the cavalry, which was made up of aristocrats (who had to supply their own horses, a major expense), nor did he fight with the poor in the lightly armed infantry. At some point in his life, Socrates did have some money. The popular depiction of him in his later years as an impoverished philosopher is not an accurate portrayal of his financial situation during the whole of his life.

When Socrates served as a hoplite in the fight against the city-state Potidaea in 432 BCE, he shared his living quarters with a young man named Alcibiades (450–404 BCE). The two formed the kind of friendship that often develops between soldiers engaged in warfare, but their bond became especially close when Socrates saved the life of his comrade, a brave act that would later come back to haunt him. During a fierce battle, Alcibiades was wounded and fell to the ground. Socrates stood over his friend and protected him from further harm despite the danger to himself.

Little did Socrates know that his heroic service in the battle at Potidaea would contribute to his death by execution three decades later. What was initially celebrated as a heroic act later became one of the chief pieces of evidence in the trial against him.

FAMILY LIFE

When he was fifty years old, Socrates married a woman named Xanthippe, and they had three sons. Xanthippe carried an infant in her arms to the prison cell where she said good-bye to Socrates. This indicates that she was probably significantly younger than Socrates, as she was still of childbearing age at the time that her seventy-one-year-old husband was condemned to death.

There are conflicting accounts as to whether Socrates and Xanthippe's household was a happy one. Some stories maintain that Socrates loved his wife for her intellect—she was said to be the only person who could get the better of her husband in a debate. Other tales paint Xanthippe as a bit of a bully and a nag. Her frustration and anger may have arisen from Socrates's choice to spend his days preaching on the streets for free instead of working at a paying job.

Several theories exist concerning how Socrates supported himself and his family with no earnings. He refused to take money from his students, a practice for which he criticized his philosophical predecessors. He may have lived off a little bit of money that his father had left him, or the family may have lived off the wealth from Xanthippe's side of the family. He probably received some gifts of money and food from his well-heeled disciples, despite his objections to the practice.

Nothing in Socrates's early life gave any indication that he would eventually give up his relatively comfortable life as a skilled tradesperson to become a penniless philosopher who walked the streets of Athens challenging strangers about their moral condition. However, this stonecutter's son would become one of the world's greatest and most influential thinkers to shape Western notions of law, ethics, and philosophy for ages to come.

PREDECESSORS AND INFLUENCES

The word *philosophy* comes from the Latin words *philos* ("love") and *sofia* ("wisdom"), so "philosophy" literally means "love of wisdom." How Socrates supported his family, and at what point in his life he gave up his stonecutters' tools, backbreaking days in the sun, and income in order to devote himself to a penniless life in search of wisdom is uncertain. But Socrates was probably introduced to philosophy by his teacher Archelaus, who encouraged him to read the works of early natural philosophers. Socrates may have had contact with some of these thinkers or their students when they passed through Athens. Today, these philosophers are known as the pre-Socratic philosophers.

PYTHAGOREANS

The pre-Socratics departed from earlier sages by trying to understand the world through logic and reason rather than with the help of religion and mythology. These philosophers turned their focus on the natural world and made claims about life, Earth, and the universe based on scientific observations and mathematics. One of the leading thinkers in this group was Pythagoras, for whom the Pythagorean branch of pre-Socratic philosophy is named.

The pre-Socratics were usually Greeks who lived outside Athens, were sometimes educated in Egypt

The philosopher Pythagoras and the Pythagorean school he founded were profoundly influential in the development of rational philosophy. Socrates was most likely influenced by the Pythagoreans, although his own teachings had some significant differences.

and Persia (modern-day Iran, where the study of math and science was far advanced), and traveled around the Mediterranean islands teaching their ideas. The pre-Socratics must have sparked Socrates's interest in philosophy, as they were the preeminent philosophers when he was a boy. At some point, he must have listened to what they had to say when they passed through Athens.

THE WISDOM-SELLERS

As a young man, Socrates also encountered another group of early thinkers called the Sophists. The Sophists were given the nickname the "wisdom-sellers" because they traveled around the Mediterranean offering to teach subjects such as rhetoric (the study of argument) and logic to anyone who was willing to pay for the instruction.

Socrates disagreed with many of the Sophists' ways of doing things. The Sophists' arguably hypocritical practice of demanding money while urging people to reconsider their values inspired Socrates's refusal to charge his students tuition. He felt he had a mission to spread virtue. And this mission was a contribution to society, not a moneymaking scheme. If he had to sacrifice a comfortable life to this noble vocation, so be it.

Socrates also disagreed with the Sophists' approach to rhetoric as a tool for persuasion. The Sophists believed that for the sake of training a student's argumentative skills, the student should take a position in a debate and argue that position tirelessly, regardless of whether the position is right or wrong or whether the student really believes in the truth of what he or she is arguing. Related to this, one of the leading Sophists, Protagoras, believed that there was no such thing as absolute and universal truth or falsehood. If something seemed true to one person, then it was true for that person. If the same thing seemed false to another person, then it was false to that person. Socrates believed that truth was both sacred and objective (not something that changed from situation to situation, or from person to person). He felt that truth should never be compromised for the sake of argument, or for anything else.

Nevertheless, later in life, Socrates was often labeled a Sophist by the Athenians, including by his own students and followers. He was similar to the Sophists in that he had little or no interest in questions relating to metaphysics, cosmology, or the physical world. Both Socrates and the Sophists were concerned mainly with ethics. They are remembered for their methods of questioning ethical beliefs, rather than providing ethical "answers" or a set of philosophical absolutes. And both were more interested in breaking down other people's moral beliefs and ideas by revealing their flaws than in providing their listeners with an alternative, improved moral system by which to live. Like the Sophists, Socrates did not always offer clear guidelines on truth and virtue. Instead, he acted as a moral critic who shook the confidence of his audience in the truth of their popularly held opinions.

SELF-EXAMINATION

Despite Socrates's ethical and philosophical differences with its practitioners, Sophism is the branch of philosophy that appears to have had the most influence in shaping Socrates's own ideas. While the Pythagoreans devoted their energy to understanding the mysteries of the universe through mysticism, mathematics, and numbers and scientific observation, Sophists sought to understand the world through the lens of morality.

The Sophists believed that people should devote themselves to the quest to define what it means to be good or virtuous and that they should use this new knowledge and understanding to change their personal conduct. They didn't believe that philosophy should exist only to spark discussion, but rather that the ideas and conclusions that come out of philosophical debate should be put to practical use to improve the lives and behaviors of individuals and their communities.

Socrates's own approach to discovering truth and virtue is perhaps best captured in the saying most commonly associated with him: "Know thyself." He believed that the path to knowledge and wisdom began by careful self-examination and that the "unexamined life is not worth living." An individual's acknowledgement of his or her own ignorance was a crucial part of this path. The origin of the expression "know thyself" is fundamental to the story of Socrates's lifelong inquiry into his own moral health and that of his fellow Athenians.

CHAPTER TWO

THE DECLINE OF ATHENS

Socrates's fate was closely tied to that of the city-state of Athens. The cultural, political, and social climate of Athens during its golden age made it a mecca of outstanding achievements in nearly every field. Magnificent architectural monuments to the gods, a democracy that gave citizens a voice, and the spirit of intellectual pursuit are just some of the inheritances of this great civilization that we still enjoy millennia later.

But Athens would not remain a thriving center forever. Although it remained at the forefront of Mediterranean culture, politics, and art for much of Socrates's life, it would once again encounter strife. By examining the rise and fall of this great civilization, the twists of fate of Socrates's own life become clearer.

AN EMPIRE FALLS TO ATHENS

The nation of Greece did not exist during Socrates's time. In ancient times, the country we now call Greece was a collection of more than one hundred small, independent city-states, or poleis. Each polis functioned as a separate nation with its own government. Athens was the biggest city-state in the fifth century BCE, with a population of 300,000 to 350,000 people. The citizens in each of these city-states swore allegiance only to their own polis, and the local customs and traditions were very different within each polis. However, the citizens of the Greek city-states shared a common written and spoken language, and they would join together for the Olympic Games and sometimes to fight a common enemy. This arrangement had been in place for about three centuries before Socrates's time.

Socrates came of age during one of the few times in Athens's history that was marked by an extended period of peace. Greece's ancient history was one of almost constant warfare, and a persistent enemy was Persia (an empire centered in modern-day Iran). Fifth-century-BCE Persia had an empire that spanned across much of the Middle East, Asia Minor, and central Asia, including some Greek colonies to the north and east of Athens. The Persian Empire had a very strong military that was used both to defend its borders and extend its territory. In 499 BCE, the Persian army attempted to conquer more Greek city-states. With Athens at the

One of the first great naval battles, the Battle of Salamis resulted in a Greek victory over Persian forces and helped turn the tide of the Persian Wars.

helm, the city-states brought under Persian control began to rebel, beginning a conflict known as the Persian Wars (499–479 BCE).

The Athenians led an alliance of Greek city-states that eventually defeated the Persians after a twenty-year war, with a final naval battle at Salamis in 480 BCE that resulted in the triumph of a badly outnumbered Athenian fleet. In 479 BCE, a Spartan king led the Greek allies in the Battle of Plataea, leading to the final retreat of the Persian forces. The allied Greek city-states declared victory, and Athens was praised as the Persian Wars' ultimate victor.

A GREAT STATESMAN EMERGES

"Future ages will wonder at us, as the present age wonders at us now." This was the accurate prediction of the statesman Pericles (495–429 BCE), uttered as he contemplated the great undertakings into which he would soon lead Athenians. Pericles, who was at the forefront of Athens's golden age, ruled from 460 BCE to 431 BCE. He was determined to go down in history as the statesman most responsible for Athens's long-lasting greatness. He eventually succeeded in this lofty goal.

Pericles was from a wealthy, aristocratic family. Like most young men, he started his military career as an ordinary soldier but rose rapidly to the post of statesman-general. Aside from his family connections, Pericles's sharp intellect and powerful personality helped him rise in the political world. Pericles's charisma and persuasive speeches

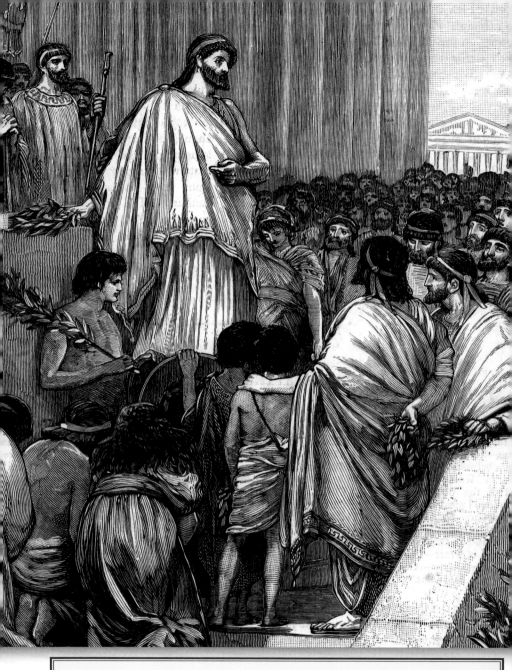

Pericles was known for his military skills, political prowess, support for the arts, and powerful oratory. He is seen here delivering his Funeral Oration during the Peloponnesian War, one of his most memorable addresses.

won over voters in election after election, and his civic proposals gained the support of his Assembly colleagues. As the strongest advocate for reforms and progress during the fifth century, Pericles is considered the visionary of Athens's golden age, an era of unparalleled achievement that may not have been possible without him.

CULTURE IN THE GOLDEN AGE

The Greek city-states were among the first societies to foster the development of an intellectual class. In Athens's case, this was partly due to the recent installation of direct democracy, the first such political system in the world. Rather than citizens electing officials to represent them, as in a representative democracy (like that of the United States today), Athens's voting citizens all had a direct voice in government at meetings that were open to the public.

Because the individual was so important in a direct democracy, and because the average citizen had an immediate influence upon public policy and decision making, Pericles believed it was important to develop a cultured, educated, and intelligent citizenry. As a result, Pericles advanced the idea that it was important for governments to invest in the arts.

During Athens's golden age, Pericles encouraged the work of scientists, musicians, and poets—almost anybody who had a talent to share. He supported talented artists with lavish government funding and encouraged their input on civic projects. One of the most monumental public projects during his reign was the building of the Parthenon, which was a temple dedicated to the goddess Athena.

Much of the Parthenon has been destroyed over the centuries, but its basic structure remains standing today. In addition to being a temple, it was once a monument to Athenian power and wealth.

The Acropolis had been damaged in the Persian Wars, and the Athenians were able to rebuild it at the same time the Parthenon was under construction,

giving further evidence of the city's abundant wealth at the time. It is rumored that Socrates contributed his skills as a stonemason during these rebuilding efforts. In addition, one of the most talented sculptors of the ancient world, Phidias (circa 500–432 BCE), lived during this time and constructed the celebrated statue of Zeus, which was designated as one of the Seven Wonders of the Ancient World.

Pericles's artistic initiatives weren't designed only to beautify the city. Political considerations were also driving forces behind the building of these monuments. Flush with victory after the Persian Wars, Pericles wanted to create impressive displays of Athenian power, and he used these projects to show off Athens's might and riches. For example, the sculptures of the Parthenon served as artistic propaganda that told the tale of Athens's military victories. The grandeur of the temple alone broadcast the superiority of Athens to all who passed by.

The golden age was a great time to be living in Athens, as long as you were a male citizen. Women were not permitted to attend school, participate in politics, or vote, and they were generally confined to the home. Male Athenian citizens had more free time to enjoy the grandeur and cultural richness of their city, due in part to slavery. Despite Athens's progressive experiments in democracy, there didn't seem to be any qualms about using slave labor or giving citizens certain rights and freedoms denied to others living in their midst. At least one-quarter of Athens's population was made up of slaves, who were usually prisoners of war. Despite its reliance on slavery and its denial of citizenship to some residents, Athens enjoyed peace and prosperity during this period. The citizens seemed happy with and trusting of their leaders. As a result, culture flourished, allowing a figure as eccentric as Socrates to emerge as Athens's most prominent thinker.

CORRUPTION IN ATHENS

After its final triumph over Persia at the Battle of Salamis, Athens founded the Delian League with many of its city-state allies. The league was a collective security alliance that offered each city-state the protection of its Greek allies from foreign invasion. Sparta was the only major Greek city-state that refused to take part in this

SLAVES

Perhaps the worst fate in the golden age of Athens was captivity and enslavement. Slaves made up a large portion of Athens's population, but they were not granted any of the rights of citizens. Many were forced to mine silver. These slaves spent long, dark days in dangerous underground tunnels. Most slaves were prisoners captured in battle, and, in some cases, kidnapped from other city-states or other Mediterranean islands. The slave was often paid for his or her services and could eventually buy his or her freedom and eventually become a metic, or resident alien.

Though they were not treated very well, slaves provided the foundation for the glories of Athens's golden age. Their labor built the city's world-famous and enduring architectural marvels, and, in an indirect way, slaves also helped establish the philosophical underpinnings of the golden age. Ironically, Athens would not have become the progressive society that it was without the contribution of slave labor, for this afforded the intellectuals the time and leisure to think about public ethics and morality. Socrates, though a harsh critic of Athenian society's morals, never questioned the institution of slavery.

joint safety net. Athens collected taxes from the league's member states and set aside this money for any necessary military campaigns in the future. In its early stages, the alliance was very active. It fought the Persians in their remaining strongholds and eventually drove them out of the Aegean and from the coasts of Asia Minor. As the Persian threat receded, however, the allies grew impatient with the constant need to contribute to the defense fund. They were no longer convinced it was necessary.

While other city-states continued to add to the fund, Athens stopped paying its share of the taxes, contributing nothing to the league's treasury for decades. In fact, the fund was used to pay for local initiatives. Pericles dipped into the defense treasury to finance city-improvement projects, including the construction of the Parthenon.

By the end of his reign, Pericles had harmed Athens nearly as much as he had helped it. His costly projects and dishonest financial dealings are blamed for bringing down the greatest glory of golden age Athens: its democratic system. Pericles's tragic flaw may have been that he lacked foresight. His plans for improving Athens didn't take into consideration a long-term view of the future. He chose not to consider how Athens's neighbors would react to the city's great show of riches, a wealth built upon theft from its allies.

WAR WITH SPARTA

Throughout Athens's golden age, the city's great enemy, Sparta—which held alliances with most of the small city-states not affiliated with Athens—was growing more and more anxious about Athens's astounding power and wealth. In 460 BCE, Sparta finally launched an attack against its rival. What followed was fifteen years of combat between the two city-states.

It had been decades since the allied Greek territories had engaged in battle with Persia, and many city-states no longer saw the Persian Empire as a threat. There was a growing movement among the city-states of the Delian League to withdraw from the alliance and stop paying taxes to Athens for protection that was no longer needed. As the city-states voiced their intention to drop out, Athens used its strong naval fleet—paid for with Delian League funds—to flex its muscle. For example, when leaders of Miletus told Athens about the city-state's intention to stop paying taxes to the league, Athens sent its navy to destroy the city.

By 431 BCE, Sparta had formed a new alliance of city-states that were angered by Athens's abuse of power and wanted to topple it from its dominant perch. Thus began a series of battles collectively known as the Peloponnesian War, which was ultimately won by Sparta.

War was not Athens's only woe, however. Under Pericles's leadership, the Athenians adopted a defensive strategy in which their navy harassed the Spartans with quick raids while their army and citizens retreated behind the city walls and refused to engage the Spartans' stronger land forces. Due to the overcrowding that resulted, Athens fell victim to a mysterious plague that eventually claimed at least 25 percent of the city's population. Pericles, along with his entire family, died from this plague in 429 BCE. Without strong leadership, Athens was in no position to continue battling the tireless and fierce Spartans.

The Peloponnesian War lasted twenty-seven years, during which time Athenian forces faced many setbacks, including a crippling defeat at Sicily, depicted here.

The final battle in the Peloponnesian War occurred in 404 BCE, and Athens was besieged and forced to surrender. Upon Athens's defeat, Sparta immediately

installed a group of Athenian nobles, known as the Thirty Tyrants, to rule over the city-state. The Thirty Tyrants embarked on a rule of terror. Led by Critias, a former associate of Socrates's, they executed 1,500 of their opponents and confiscated their property. Stunned by this unprecedented violence, the pro-democratic Athenians fled into exile. They organized a resistance and retook part of the city, as all-out war broke out. Sparta stepped in to declare an amnesty (an official declaration of peace and forgiveness) and restored democracy in 403 BCE. Though the Athenians had regained their government, the Pericles era of Athenian intellectualism, achievement, and power had ended. Athenians were bitter and demoralized, and their city would never again enjoy a period of such dominance, influence, and creative flowering.

The fate of Athens mirrored—and in many ways shaped—that of one of its greatest philosophers. Socrates was born not long after Athens triumphed in the Persian Wars and would be executed only a few years after Athens suffered its staggering loss to Sparta. At a time of immense intellectual flourishing in the city, Socrates's contributions would stand out. But as Athens sought to regain a sense of stability in the wake of its defeat, Socrates's radical teachings could have no home.

CHAPTER THREE

THE MAKING OF A PHILOSOPHER

ncient Greeks would often turn to their gods in times of need, for matters great or small. The words of the gods were communicated at sacred sites by way of oracles—priests or priestesses who received divine messages (also called oracles) and delivered them to visitors who had questions or requests. One of the most visited shrines was at Delphi. Chaerephon, a friend of Socrates's, would embark on a journey to Delphi himself, around the time that Socrates was thirty years old. Chaerephon would receive a divine message that would shape Socrates's philosophical teachings and guide him throughout the remainder of his life.

AN UNUSUAL PILGRIMAGE

Chaerephon went to Delphi with a particular question in mind. He asked the oracle whether there was anybody wiser

Pilgrims to Delphi would receive oracles from the Pythia, or priestess, who would engage in several rituals, including drinking from a sacred spring and chewing laurel leaves, before delivering her message.

than Socrates. The oracle declared that Socrates was the wisest man of all time. At first, when Chaerephon reported the oracle's reply to his friend, the modest Socrates was bewildered. He was absolutely sure that he was not wise, much less the wisest of all, and wondered why the oracle would make such a false statement. He was determined to understand the exact meaning of the prophecy, and he asked himself question after question until he arrived at a conclusion that made sense to him.

Socrates decided that the oracle must have meant that he was the wisest person precisely because he alone knew and admitted to himself that he was not wise. The only way in which he was wiser than other people was that he knew something about himself that they didn't know about themselves—that he was an ignorant man who knew absolutely nothing except the fact of his own ignorance.

It is unclear what the status of Socrates's career was at the time of Chaerephon's pilgrimage—whether he was already steeped in philosophical inquiry and engaged in

THE ORACLE AT DELPHI

In the seventh century BCE, a temple to Apollo, the god of music and arts, was built on the southern slope of Mount Parnassus in the town of Delphi—a place once thought to be the center of the world. The temple had been destroyed and rebuilt twice by the third century BCE. People traveled from far and wide to present their offerings of gold and get their questions answered by the Pythia, a priestess of Apollo. The Pythia had to be at least fifty years old and was required to live in seclusion near the temple. On the day she gave oracles, usually once a month, she would undergo a cleansing ritual that ancient Greeks believed put her into a trance. Priests were present at Delphi to translate her prophecies to visitors.

Government leaders would send gifts to be placed at the temple in exchange for Apollo's protection of their city-states. As a result, Delphi eventually became a marvelous showplace for art and other treasures. In the fourth century CE, after Greece converted to Christianity, all oracles around the Mediterranean were silenced. Over time, looters raided and stole the treasures housed at the spots once considered sacred by the Greeks.

In addition to the temple of Apollo, Delphi was home to the Sanctuary of Athena, the remains of which are seen here. Visitors today are still drawn to the ruins of both shrines.

teaching, or whether the oracle's proclamation prompted his abandonment of stonework for the life of the mind. What is known is that the oracle's declaration played a major role in Socrates's life. It served as the inspiration for his famous approach to philosophical inquiry—the so-called Socratic method.

CREATING HIS GREATEST LEGACY

Unlike many of the philosophers who are well known and studied today, Socrates did not have a core set of beliefs that he taught and sought to explain. Socrates's actual ideas were not his greatest legacy. In fact, little of his actual philosophy has come down to us. What did make him famous, however, was his method of questioning, which he developed as he puzzled over the oracle's prophecy. This process—now called the Socratic method—was designed to gain understanding of difficult philosophical problems that did not necessarily have clear-cut answers. He believed that through the asking of a carefully constructed series of questions, a person could reach solid conclusions. At the very least, the questions could bring to the surface the confusions, contradictions, and errors at the heart of the conventional ethical beliefs of most Athenians.

Socrates compared these question-and-answer dialogues to the work of a midwife. He said that his questions gave birth to his debate partner's definitions and ideas. Socrates himself never took a position. Rather, he simply exposed the errors of other people's conventional, unexamined assumptions and encouraged them to formulate a more correct view. In this way, Socrates aided the development of other people's ideas, but the people who engaged in debates with him did most of the work by pushing their ideas to the surface in response to his questions.

The purpose of the Socratic method was to get people to raise ethical questions and come up with answers for themselves, rather than blindly accept the morality handed down to them by their political and religious leaders or by society. He wanted to shake people out of their belief that they already knew everything. If he could

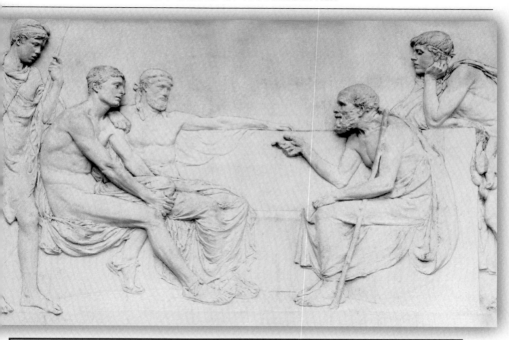

*This bas-relief depicts Socrates (*second from the right*) engaged in discussion with several other men. Socrates's unorthodox method of questioning ideas and ethics attracted many followers.*

make them confront the fact that they didn't know very much after all, they would then be better able to acquire real knowledge.

The Socratic method was a two-part process. Socrates would begin by pretending to know little about whatever was being discussed, asking questions of his pupils in order to learn something. Feeling flattered by Socrates's apparent respect for their intelligence and knowledge, and perhaps made a little overconfident as a result, they would often assert positions that were built upon flawed premises. Socrates's volley of questions would soon expose his pupils' ignorance and force them to admit the error of their opinions. This is known as the destructive part of the process.

Having identified and rejected the flawed opinions, Socrates would then move to a new series of questions designed to make his pupils develop new, more well-thought-out opinions about the subject being discussed. This is known as the constructive part of the process. These improved opinions were usually the end result of Socrates urging his students, through his questions, to arrive at definitions of the subject being discussed and thereby achieve knowledge.

Socrates believed that right conduct depended upon clear knowledge. For example, he believed that by defining virtue, we are better equipped to acquire virtue and become virtuous. Going even further, he felt that simply arriving at a definition for virtue was a virtue in itself. Socrates believed that virtue is knowledge, and that knowledge is virtue. It follows that various kinds of things we label as virtues, such as justice, courage, self-control, and piety, are also forms of wisdom, or knowledge. The possession of these forms of wisdom makes one a virtuous person. If one knows what is good, one will do what is good.

Socrates referred to his method of truth-seeking as *elenchus*, which translates as "cross-examination." It gave rise in the Western world to a kind of philosophical inquiry known as dialectic—the arrival at truth by exposing one's idea to opposing positions and modifying it as a result of the debate. It was through the Socratic method that Socrates came to an understanding not only of the oracle's grand prophecy but also other, more universal moral and ethical truths.

As Socrates rose to prominence, he became both the object of admiration and the target of ridicule. The message of the oracle had given him direction and shaped how he spent his days. Through his conversations and teachings, he gained a large and enthusiastic audience. But many viewed him with skepticism, distrust, or envy. A powerful few in Athens's elite sought to protect their power, and when Socrates openly disagreed with aspects of the Athenian government, they retaliated. It was the accusations of this group that would lead to Socrates's downfall.

CHAPTER FOUR

A Self-Proclaimed Gadfly

Sometimes seen as a nurturing teacher and revolutionary thinker, and sometimes as an overbearing and arrogant intellectual, Socrates was a controversial and contradictory figure. In public, he strived to maintain a humble image, wearing shabby robes and often walking around barefoot. He rejected material comforts in favor of intellectual pursuits. When the oracle proclaimed him the wisest man, he could not immediately accept that statement as true.

However, there is evidence that Socrates may not have been as modest as his appearance would indicate. Although he questioned the oracle's message, he ultimately accepted it to be a divine message from the gods, directing him to develop the spirit of philosophical inquiry in others. He refused to engage in public matters,

Despite his appearance, Socrates gained an audience with Aspasia, an intellectual and the companion of Pericles. Socrates was said to have viewed Aspasia as his own teacher in rhetoric.

saying that instead, he had to serve the gods by dedicating himself to making "inquisition into the wisdom of any one, whether citizen or stranger." By his own admission, Socrates even seems to have delighted in guiding people to admit that they were not wise, in a way validating his own position as the one chosen by the gods as wisest. Despite inspiring admiration in numerous followers, his often abrasive approach to his calling would turn one too many influential leaders against him.

ENLIGHTENING THE PUBLIC

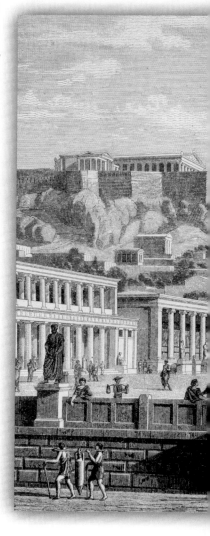

Socrates felt it was his duty to share the oracle at Delphi's revelation that each and every human being was hopelessly ignorant (or at least, uninformed and unwise). The agora, or marketplace, was the place to which he took this harsh message. Athenians became the targets of Socrates's relentless method of questioning, which was used to underscore their ignorance.

As people went about their daily business in the agora, Socrates felt it was his duty to engage those he encountered, asking them about their moral beliefs. He

This rendering depicts what the agora in Athens, where Socrates often initiated his discussions with strangers, might have looked like. It was a commercial center that also had religious, political, and social significance.

would use his roundabout Socratic method to reveal the flaws or weaknesses in his opponent's position and usually win the debates. He would take his debater's statements and question the validity and logic behind their premises. Usually his opponent would end up retracting his statements or rethinking the premises that supported them. Often, Socrates drew a crowd of eager listeners when he was engaged in these types of philosophical contests. He had a huge following of pupils in Athens, made up of curious young minds, leaders in the making, and men with a great deal of power and money.

Socrates was not trying to be mean-spirited in his attacks upon people's logic and beliefs. He just believed that if a person had come upon a good understanding of morality, it was his or her responsibility to share it with the community and convince community members of its truth and value. Naturally not everybody took to Socrates's aggressive style of teaching, nor did they want to accept his claim that they were merely ignorant beings.

WAS SOCRATES MENTALLY ILL?

Today, some mental health experts believe that Socrates may have suffered from mental illness. It was common for him to stand in contemplation in a catatonic state (motionless and expressionless), in which he would be as still as a statue and would remain in that position for hours. This is a symptom of a type of mental disorder known as schizophrenia, which affects the body's motor system, so that a sort of stupor, trance, or frozen rigidity strikes the sufferer. A less severe diagnosis is that he may have had a form of epilepsy, which causes sufferers to stare into space, unaware of their surroundings, for anywhere from several minutes to a few hours.

Socrates was not completely unaware of his tendency to "space out." In fact, he may have relished these episodes. At his trial, Socrates referred to his daemon, a sort of supernatural guiding spirit. He claimed that this daemon warned him of events that were potentially disastrous and urged him either to take a certain action or refrain from one in order to avoid trouble. This is not unlike the voices that some schizophrenics say they hear, often alerting them to imaginary dangers and threats.

In ancient times, people believed that diseases such as epilepsy were of divine origin. Their victims, the ancients believed, were inhabited by a divine force and therefore possessed mysterious and extraordinary powers. The slightly arrogant and self-aggrandizing Socrates probably didn't mind being diagnosed with such a condition.

Socrates was well aware that his relentless questioning was not always appreciated. He even called himself Athens's "gadfly," a person who persistently pesters others through criticism, like a fly that annoys with buzzing and biting. Ultimately, however, he didn't care what others thought about him. Notorious for his unattractive appearance, he is often depicted in sculptures and paintings as having a pug nose and stocky frame. He was not in the habit of bathing or shaving. His round stomach protruded from the loose robes he wore, and he walked around the agora barefoot. Socrates was considered an oddball and eccentric among the refined and cultured Athenians of his time.

THE QUEST FOR VIRTUE

The core of Socrates's philosophy was his belief that virtue could be gained through knowledge. Conversely, he believed that a person who does wrong is simply lacking in knowledge and acting out of ignorance. People do not do wrong on purpose. This is why Socrates chose to devote his life to educating his fellow citizens. If he taught Athenians through the posing of moral questions designed to make them examine their moral system, then they would eventually gain the knowledge needed to lead more moral lives. They would learn how to do right in every situation.

Socrates believed that although people did not mean to do harm, their ignorance nevertheless fueled bad deeds. His lifelong quest to define goodness and truth was undertaken in the belief that if a person could define what was wrong, then he or she would know how to act morally. Socrates believed that if people could correctly define morality and immorality, then they would almost always act according to what was right. But how can one arrive at an absolute definition of right and wrong, one that doesn't change regardless of the specific circumstances? Socrates's dialogues attempted to tackle this problem of moral complexity and relativity.

In Socrates's quest to understand and define difficult and debatable concepts, such as truth, knowledge, and right and wrong, he formed friendships, created a following, irritated strangers, and made many enemies throughout Athens. Socrates's fatal mistake was that he would question passersby without discrimination or regard to their sensitivities or position in society. Some of the victims of his verbal assaults were powerful officials who did not want to lose face to a man they took to be the town's raving eccentric. Some Athenian leaders and parents of his young followers disliked Socrates's irksome nature so much that when Athens's golden age began to darken, they turned their rage against a convenient target—the old barefooted gadfly of Athens.

ATHENS'S SCAPEGOAT

As the fifth century turned into the fourth century BCE, the atmosphere in Athens became inhospitable to a character like Socrates. After the end of the golden

age, the tolerant citizens of
Athens who had once accepted
Socrates—and perhaps even
encouraged his confrontational
philosophical passion—turned
suspicious and restrictive.
Athenians were saddened by
the death of their great leader
Pericles, worn out from years
of war and plague, and anxious
about their city's uncertain
future. Athens was surrounded
by an atmosphere of instability,
and Athenian society was
nothing like the progressive,
forward-looking one it had
been only a few years before.
Athenian leaders, rather than
looking to the future for ways
to improve their city, turned
their attention instead to
the past to find someone or
something to blame for their
recent misfortunes.

Socrates, the highly
public annoyance, became a
target of Athenian anger and
scapegoating. He was a well-
known figure around Athens, but not necessarily a well-
liked one, and in many ways he was a quintessential product

The leader of the Thirty Tyrants, Critias—seen here speaking—was a follower of Socrates and a relative of Plato. Socrates's association with Critias and his anti-democratic leanings turned many in Athens against him.

of the golden age that had recently ended in disgrace and defeat. Despite the fact that Athenians had lost control of their city and saw a huge portion of their population sicken and die with an unexplainable disease, Socrates carried on as he always had. He remained the calm, cool, single-minded philosopher who agitated Athenians by bullying them into conversations about public morality and private matters of the soul.

This man, who was famous for his loud and public tirades, remained uncharacteristically silent about the huge changes that were sweeping over Athens. To his enemies, the philosophical probing that Socrates had been carrying on for several decades—which was often undeniably critical, contrary, and antidemocratic—was now seen as disrespectful, unpatriotic, and increasingly intolerable.

Socrates's political views had always been out of step with the mainstream thought of Athens. As the preeminent thinker during Athens's golden age, Socrates used his prominence to freely voice his doubts about the Athenians' beloved democracy. He questioned the wisdom of having a government in which a common person could become the nation's ruler and a state in which the ruled could also serve as the rulers. He also questioned the wisdom of people making important state decisions while being subject to the whims of a restless voting public. Instead, Socrates said that major governmental decisions should be made by "the one who knows," implying that he thought a single ruler, such as a king, should wield the power of the government. He is quoted in *Memorabilia* as saying, "The one who knows should rule, and the others obey." This kind of system was similar to Sparta's government of the Thirty Tyrants imposed upon Athens after the Peloponnesian War.

When Athens's democratic government seemed to be indestructible, Socrates's political opinions were tolerated, even if dismissed by the city's leaders. But shaken by disease and defeat, Athenians increasingly shied away from his revolutionary ideas, seeking stability and the tools to regain what they had lost. In an effort to undermine the still influential and unconventional ideas of Socrates, an obscure poet would soon emerge to lead the charge against him.

CHAPTER FIVE

SOCRATES ON TRIAL

How could such a once prosperous city turn so quickly and dramatically on the man that gave it some of its most important intellectual legacies? Part of the answer lies in the disillusionment of some powerful Athenian leaders. When Sparta imposed its rule of the Thirty Tyrants over Athens following the Peloponnesian War, many Athenian politicians were embittered by the experience and sought retaliation. After the Tyrants' leader Critias was killed in battle, many of those who served as Athenian democratic leaders before the war returned to power and looked for opportunities for retribution.

One such leader was named Anytus. But after the fall of Critias, there were few Spartans left in Athens to target. So Anytus turned his gaze to the rude, irreverent, antidemocratic critic

Like many Athenians, Anytus, seen here, targeted Socrates and blamed him for Athens's problems. Although Socrates's association with Critias was not included in the charges against him, it likely played a part in his trial.

holding fort at the agora—Socrates. Anytus enlisted a poet friend, Meletus, to do his dirty work for him. Calling in a favor owed to him, Anytus urged Meletus to file charges against Socrates with the Athenian courts, fearing that if he did it himself, he would fall out of favor with Athenian voters if he lost. Anytus reasoned that if Meletus lost the case instead, it would not matter because he was relatively unknown. In 399 BCE, Meletus brought two charges against Socrates. The first accused him of "corrupting" the youth of Athens. The second charged the philosopher with "not worshipping the gods worshipped by the state." This second charge may have been inspired by Socrates's supposed belief that he was guided by a personal divine spirit. Both crimes were punishable by death.

GUILTY BY ASSOCIATION

In his days spent walking around Athens, Socrates engaged in dialogues with many different people and formed friendships with men from all walks of life. The company a person kept was not at issue during the open-minded golden age, but it did become a matter of scrutiny during the more fearful and repressive era that followed the loss to Sparta at the beginning of the fourth century. A few decades earlier, Socrates had befriended three men whose friendships would come to haunt him at the turn of the century. Two of these men were soldiers who would go down in history as being primarily responsible for bringing Athens's golden age to an end.

One of these destructive friendships was formed when Socrates was serving in the Athenian army during a war with the city-state Potidaea in 432 BCE. During a battle, Socrates saved the life of his fellow soldier Alcibiades. Out of gratitude and respect, Alcibiades became a fervent follower of Socrates. He was often seen following the old sage around the agora, drawing the attention of Socrates's enemies. This ardent disciple of Socrates's is known today as the Benedict Arnold of Greece (named after the famous defector from the Continental army during the American Revolution [1775–1783] whose name became synonymous with "traitor").

Alcibiades was once a popular liberal politician in Athens's Assembly, but during the Peloponnesian War, Alcibiades secretly switched his allegiance to Sparta. In 415 BCE, he took advantage of his power in the Assembly and the trust Athenians had placed in him by proposing a plan to invade the rich and powerful city-state Syracuse. He argued that the invasion would increase Athens's resources in the war against Sparta. In 413 BCE, however, before the Athenians reached Syracuse, Alcibiades and the well-prepared and informed Spartan troops ambushed the surprised Athenians, killing tens of thousands of them.

Following the restoration of the Athenian government, Socrates suffered for his association with Alcibiades. To make matters worse for him, before the Peloponnesian War, Alcibiades had been accused of defacing religious statues. Socrates had nothing to do with either Alcibiades's treason or his vandalism, and

In this work, Socrates (seated) reprimands Alcibiades. Although Socrates did not agree with his friend and disciple's decision to support Sparta over Athens, their association furthered the charge that Socrates corrupted Athens's youth.

would surely have condemned both. In the courtroom, however, Meletus reminded the jurors of Socrates's ties to this sacrilegious traitor of Athens, hinting that Socrates was guilty by association. He even implied that Socrates may have been the one to urge Alcibiades to turn against his own country during the Peloponnesian War.

Another of Socrates's unfortunate acquaintances was with a former disciple named Critias. Like Alcibiades, Critias would go down in history as a traitor to Athens during the Peloponnesian War and during his tenure as a major leader in the pro-Spartan Thirty Tyrants government. Unlike Alcibiades, Critias died in the battle in which the Thirty Tyrants lost control of Athens and couldn't be punished for his treachery.

Xenophon was the third man whose friendship compromised Socrates's standing in society and made him vulnerable to his enemies' attacks. He was an Athenian who became notorious for his lack of loyalty. He came from a wealthy family and was a member of the cavalry near the end of the Peloponnesian War. Like other members of this elite service, he probably sided with the Thirty Tyrants during the civil war. In 401 BCE, he joined an expedition of Greek mercenaries (soldiers for hire), who were hired to help Cyrus the Younger seize the Persian crown from his brother. Socrates urged him not to go, since Cyrus was perceived as a friend of the Spartans and an enemy of Athens. Xenophon ignored his advice and went anyway. His disloyal action thus seemed to confirm the corrupting effects of Socrates's teaching on the young and probably helped convict his teacher when he faced charges in 399 BCE.

Against the advice of Socrates, Xenophon joined a group of Greek mercenaries, called the Ten Thousand, who helped Cyrus the Younger in battle against his brother. They are seen here after the Battle of Cunaxa.

He once joined in a battle fought against the Athenians during the Persian Wars and was later exiled for his efforts on behalf of the enemy. While in exile, he went

to Sparta, Athens's greatest enemy, and spent much of his time traveling from city-state to city-state, joining various battles on behalf of various nations, while developing no lasting ties to any one government. During one of these campaigns, Xenophon found himself fighting alongside his former countrymen, the Athenians. In exchange for his services, he was granted permission to return to his birthplace. He declined to take advantage of the offer.

DRIVEN BY FEAR

Anytus used these skeletons in Socrates's closet to bolster the case against him, but what really inspired Anytus's accusations was his concern for the future of Athens. What Anytus actually meant by his accusations was that

ATHENIAN COURTS

During the time of Socrates's trial, any citizen in Athens could file charges against another person for any kind of wrongdoing. There were no lawyers or prosecutors. Instead, the plaintiff (the person bringing the charges) and defendant each argued their own case. Juries were made up of male citizens who were chosen from a pool of candidates. Unlike the American jury system today, in which the jury unanimously decides the verdict, the jurors in an Athenian court each cast their own vote, with the majority vote deciding the defendant's fate. Juries were usually made up of at least a few hundred people to minimize the chances of a large number of jurists being bribed by either the plaintiff or the defendant.

Socrates was corrupting the young politically, rather than morally (though he did object to Socrates's quoting of somewhat lewd passages from Homer and Hesiod). In Anytus's eyes, the widespread adoption of Socrates's views among Athenian youth would represent a grave threat to the city-state's future. Socrates himself was not a threat to Athens's democracy, as he was seventy-one years old and penniless at the time these accusations were being made, but his ideas were.

Anytus was concerned that Socrates was broadcasting his antidemocratic views to Athens's youth, with his criticisms of Athenian institutions and popular elections. He also felt that Socrates urged his pupils to disobey their parents (and perhaps, by extension, Athenian rulers as well) and accept his authority instead. Anytus feared that these young Athenians would adopt and spread their teacher's views long after Socrates's death. This was the real motivation behind his attempts to silence the philosopher permanently before he could win over and influence any more young minds.

THE *APOLOGY* OF SOCRATES

A record of Socrates's trial appears in Plato's *Apology*, which was written long after the proceedings. According to Plato's account, in the summer of 399 BCE, during which the trial was held, Socrates was at the height of his persuasive powers. Realizing that the trial might represent one of his last opportunities to address a large audience, the eloquent and verbose Socrates took full advantage of the occasion.

Socrates used his trial not only as an opportunity to defend himself against Meletus's charges but also as a platform for the spread of his philosophy. In order to effectively launch an effective defense of his moral character and make a mockery of Meletus and his accusations, Socrates began his testimony with a show of humility, apologizing that his testimony would likely sound familiar to his listeners. He also emphasized his

Socrates, depicted here defending himself during his trial, used his trial as an opportunity to attack his accusers, expound on his philosophy, and demonstrate both his eloquence and his innocence.

innocence by mentioning his lack of familiarity with trial proceedings.

> I must beg of you to grant me one favor, which is this—If you hear me using the same words in my defence which I have been in the habit of using, and which most of you may have heard in the agora, and at the tables of the money-changers, or anywhere else, I would ask you not to be surprised at this, and not to interrupt me. For I am more than seventy years of age, and this is the first time that I have ever appeared in a court of law. . . Think only of the justice of my cause, and give heed to that: let the judge decide justly and the speaker speak truly (as quoted in *The Republic and Other Works*).

Socrates turned the courtroom into a forum for humiliating his accuser by showing the baselessness of Meletus's accusations and the foolishness of his character. In effect, he turned the tables on Meletus and threw his accuser on the defensive.

> He says that I am a doer of evil, who corrupt the youth; but I say, O men of Athens, that Meletus is a doer of evil, and the evil is that he makes a joke of a serious matter, and is too ready at bringing other men to trial from a pretended zeal and interest about matters in which he really never had the smallest interest (as quoted in *The Republic and Other Works*).

PLATO'S *APOLOGY*

Plato's *Apology* is one of his most important early dialogues. This work recounts the details of Socrates's trial and the speech he made in his defense. (The word *apology* here is used to mean a defense or explanation and is not an expression of Socrates's remorse.) Plato himself is featured as a member of the audience—which is noteworthy because he is otherwise never seen as an eyewitness to Socrates's conversations in any of his dialogues. Xenophon, another student of Socrates's, also wrote about the trial, but Plato's version is more widely accepted, as he is believed to have been present during the proceedings.

Although we cannot determine how closely *Apology* captures exactly what was actually said during the trial and how much of it reflected Plato's desire to defend or portray a particular image of his teacher, Plato's account raises questions of political, ethical, and philosophical significance. Throughout *Apology*, we see Socrates's dedication to promoting virtue by way of knowledge and questioning—the very acts that had sparked the charges against him in the first place. At the expense of his reputation, his family, and ultimately his life, he believed he should serve the public interest—even that of a public set against him—by encouraging in people curiosity and the act of inquiry.

To rebut, or contradict, the claims that he was spreading corruption among Athens's youth, Socrates employed his famous Socratic method. He began by asking Meletus whether good people do their neighbors good, and if so, then do bad people spread evil to their neighbors. Meletus believed both propositions were true. Then the philosopher asked Meletus if he believed that his corruption of youth was intentional. Meletus believed that it was.

Now Socrates had Meletus exactly where he wanted him. The philosopher used his accuser's replies to prove his own point. He said that if he were truly successful in the corruption of youth, then the youth would have become bad. He would have become aware of this because, as a neighbor to youths, he would be harmed by their evil, since Meletus agreed that bad people spread evil. However, Socrates claimed that he was not aware of having been harmed by any of his young neighbors. Socrates then drew the conclusion that either he did not corrupt anybody or he did so unintentionally. In either scenario, Socrates would be cleared of what he was being accused of: that he corrupted youth and did so deliberately.

Socrates discredited the second accusation brought against him regarding his worship practices by revealing Meletus's ignorance in the matter. The charge claimed that Socrates worshipped gods that were not deemed acceptable by the state. Socrates trapped Meletus into calling him an atheist, or a person who doesn't believe in any god. If Socrates was an atheist as Meletus claimed, then Socrates did not worship any gods, including those to which Athens objected.

Ancient Greeks worshipped many gods, including Poseidon, Zeus, and Hercules, seen here. Socrates used his trial to demonstrate that the accusation that he both worshipped unacceptable gods and was an atheist were contradictory.

Therefore, Socrates was not guilty of the claim that he worshipped gods deemed unacceptable to Athens.

Throughout his trial, Socrates's arguments were well thought out, aggressive, and sharply focused, but he also adopted a tone of joviality as he effortlessly contradicted each of the accusations he faced and made Meletus appear more and more foolish while doing so. But as he reached the conclusion of his testimony, Socrates's tone turned serious. He shifted his attention away from insulting Meletus to talking about matters of the soul with his captive audience. He urged his fellow citizens to make the improvement of their souls a priority above all others. "I do nothing but go about persuading you all, old and young alike, not to take thought for your persons or your properties, but first and chiefly to care about the greatest improvement of the soul" (as quoted in *The Republic and Other Works*).

Socrates's final words to the jury were his most contemplative and glum, as if he had a premonition of his fate. "The hour of departure has arrived, and we go our ways—I to die, and you to live. Which is better God only knows" (as quoted in *The Republic and Other Works*). Although the verdict had not been given, Socrates's pessimism was proved correct. Out of 500 jurors, 280 found Socrates guilty as charged. He was sentenced to be executed.

The verdict demonstrated an unfortunate reality of Athenian society. In word, Athenians elevated the ideals of democracy and free speech. But in practice, they could not tolerate the musings of even one man when they strayed from the accepted norms of society. In many ways, the trial was not really an indictment of Socrates's wayward habits or personal beliefs. It was really a rejection of the true exchange—and spread—of ideas, especially those that questioned institutional practices or forced people to confront uncomfortable realities and differences. In short, it was a rejection of true free speech.

CHAPTER SIX

SOCRATES'S EXECUTION AND LEGACY

ocrates did not fight the judgment and seemed resigned to accept his punishment. After an Athenian trial, the convicted party was allowed to propose an alternate (more lenient) punishment. However, when Socrates had that chance, instead of proposing a lesser penalty that would have spared his life, he brashly suggested that he receive a reward for the good he had done for Athens throughout his life, both as a soldier and a public ethicist. He requested that the state support him for the remainder of his life by giving him free meals and a place to live in the Prytaneum, a sort of community center in Athens. The request was intentionally preposterous—Socrates knew that the jury would never agree to it.

The jurists were so offended by his flippant attitude that when Socrates did suggest an alternate penalty—a fine for his offenses—they refused to waive the death sentence. Socrates did not seem to be shaken by this. He accepted the jury's decision and said that he was satisfied with his own behavior. He viewed the prospect of death with great equanimity. He wondered if there was an afterlife and said that if there was, he looked forward to the opportunity to quiz the heroic and wise men of antiquity who had lived and died before him. No matter what lay ahead after his execution, Socrates believed death would be a greater good than earthly life.

ETHICAL TO THE END

Socrates had a second chance to avoid death when his friend and pupil Crito urgently came into Socrates's prison cell at the break of dawn on the day he was to die, about thirty days after the end of the trial. He told his mentor of a plan that he and a few other friends had arranged: they had pooled their money and were planning to use it to bribe prison guards to allow their friend to sneak out and flee Athens. Socrates, with his characteristic stubbornness, objected.

Socrates argued that he made an implied contract with Athens by choosing to live in the city-state his whole life. Consequently, he felt he must abide by its laws and the decisions of its people, regardless of whether he found them to be just. He argued that it would be wrong to escape his death sentence by conveniently breaking this contract with Athens when its laws didn't serve his personal interests.

According to Greek mythology, the ferryman, Charon, transports the souls of the departed in a boat from the land of the living to the land of the dead over the rivers Styx and Acheron.

When Crito argued that thoughts of his children's future should compel Socrates to escape, the old philosopher voiced his faith that his friends would take care of them. He said that whether he went into exile or

was executed, he would not be present to raise his sons. Crito, though saddened by the idea of losing his teacher, knew that Socrates was too headstrong to be persuaded. Socrates's further words confirmed this assumption:

Think not of life and children first, and of justice afterwards, but of justice first, that you may be justified before the princes of the world below. For neither will you nor any that belong to you be happier or holier or juster in this life, or happier in another, if you do as Crito bids. Now you depart in innocence, a sufferer and not a doer of evil; a victim, not of the laws, but of men.

But if you go forth, returning evil for evil, and injury for injury, breaking the covenants and agreements which you have made with us, and wronging those whom you ought least to wrong…we shall be angry with you while you live (as quoted in *The Republic and Other Works*).

Socrates was determined to do what was right, even if that meant accepting an unjust conviction without complaint and submitting to a death sentence that was undeserved. To attempt to evade Athenian law, no matter how badly applied, would be like attacking the city-state and each of its citizens.

FINAL DAYS

Socrates did not seem afraid of death. In his last days on earth, he continued to carry on as he always had, with his thoughts focused on questions of morality. He was constantly surrounded by crowds of people who would visit him at the prison. He did not seem frightened, anxious, bitter, or angry. Socrates appeared as he always had: contemplative, calm, and eager for conversation. On the morning that Socrates was to die, he seemed to be in good spirits. He even made a joke with Crito about his chatty tendencies hours before he was to drink the deadly hemlock (a poison derived from the hemlock plant, which is in the carrot family). Crito reported to Socrates:

"The attendant who is to give you the poison has been telling me that you are not to talk much,

The poison that Socrates was forced to drink was derived from the hemlock plant, pictured here. Although the poison is actually found in the seeds, the whole plant is dangerous.

PLATO'S *PHAEDO*

Four of Plato's dialogues provide us with insight into Socrates's last days. *Euthyphro* and *Apology* discuss the time leading up to Socrates's trial and the events of the proceedings, respectively. *Crito* recounts Socrates's conversation with Crito when the latter attempts to help Socrates escape. What we know about Socrates's last day before execution is contained in Plato's *Phaedo*.

Phaedo is a dialogue between Socrates's student Phaedo, who was with his teacher the day before he was executed, and another philosopher, Echecrates. Throughout the dialogue, we learn Socrates's views about suicide, the soul, afterlife, knowledge, and scientific examinations. What makes the dialogue particularly significant is that it reveals Plato's own philosophies. For this reason, it is considered a departure from his early dialogues, which centered around Socrates's views on ethics, and is instead part of Plato's middle dialogues.

and he wants me to let you know this; for that by talking, heat is increased, and this interferes with the action of the poison; those who excite themselves are sometimes obliged to drink the poison two or three times."

"Then," said Socrates, "let him mind his business and be prepared to give the poison two or three times" (as quoted in *The Republic and Other Works*).

Socrates's engagement in philosophical discussions right up to the time of his death and his calmness before he was to drink the cup of poison underscore the sincerity of his lifelong pursuit of truth and his faith in the supreme importance of morality:

The difficulty, my friends, is not to avoid death, but to avoid immorality; for that runs faster than death. I am old and move slowly, and the slower runner (that is, death) has overtaken me, while my accusers are keen and quick, and immorality, an even faster runner, has overtaken them (as quoted in Don Nardo's *The Trial of Socrates*).

Convinced that he had done right and would continue to do so by submitting to Athenian law, Socrates had no fear of death. His critics, however, were immoral according to Socrates. Therefore, they might not be so lucky in the afterlife.

SOCRATES BIDS FAREWELL

Socrates was surrounded by many of his friends in the prison cell on the day he was to die. His wife, Xanthippe, was also there with their infant son, but Socrates ordered her to leave before he drank the poison so he wouldn't have to hear her cries.

The mood in the prison cell was somber and contemplative. The philosopher's friends first talked about Aesop's fables. Then Socrates asked Crito to help him pay a debt of a rooster that he owed to a healer. Later, as the time appointed for Socrates to drink the poison approached, Socrates shared his philosophies on the soul and its eternal nature with his good friends who were in the cell with him:

And is it likely that the soul will be blown away and destroyed immediately after leaving the body? That can never happen ... I say that the soul, itself invisible, departs for the invisible world—to the divine and immortal and rational realm, released from the error and folly of men, their fears and wild passions and all other human ills, and dwells forever in the company of gods (as quoted in *The Trial of Socrates*).

Before Socrates was served the hemlock, he asked a prison worker what he should do after consuming the poison. Socrates was told that he should walk around his cell until he felt numbness in his legs, at which time he should lie down and close his eyes.

Socrates did exactly as the jailer advised. Soon after lying down, Socrates passed away. He gave every indication of having died peacefully. The state of Athens had successfully condemned, silenced, and killed its gadfly.

IMMEDIATE AFTERMATH

There is little doubt that Socrates's death was unjust. In many ways, Socrates was a man truly dedicated to his city, despite his antidemocratic ideas. Though Socrates didn't support Athens's democratic government, when the city demanded his services in the army, he fought bravely for it. And when Athens condemned him to die, he obediently accepted the punishment without feeling any bitterness. When he had the chance to evade his death sentence, he refused on the grounds that he must remain loyal to the alliance he made with his city-state, even if that meant submitting to an unjust punishment.

If Socrates was guilty of anything, it was being an annoying intellectual and bullying moralist with an abrasive personality, eccentric mannerisms, and antidemocratic views. Later generations of Greeks and members of other Western cultures saw Socrates's condemnation, conviction, and execution as a tragic breach of justice and a shameful failure of democracy. But in Athens, Socrates's death caused no great outcry and no immediate changes to society. Life carried on as usual. Indeed, Anytus, the politician behind the charges against Socrates, rose even further in popularity and power.

Socrates was seen as someone who wanted to shake up Athenian tradition. As a result, he became associated with the waves of change—most of it distressing, destructive, and disastrous—that had swamped Athens since the end of Pericles's reign. To help Athens return to its former glory, this agent of change had to be destroyed.

Gaetano Gandolfi's The Death of Socrates *portrays Socrates surrounded by friends and followers in his prison cell shortly before his death.*

A THINKER FOR THE AGES

In the end, it was Athens that fostered the gadfly's eccentricities and his philosophical ideas, and then punished him for them. And, paradoxically, it was Athens's execution of Socrates that helped preserve his memory and enshrine his passionate commitment to knowledge, truth, ethics—to always knowing and doing what is right.

Plato, Socrates's most famous pupil, dedicated himself to preserving this legacy of his mentor. He traveled through Greece, Italy, and Egypt in an effort to understand morals and political justice. He later returned to Athens and established a school called the Academy, which was dedicated to promoting scholarship in philosophy and other subjects using the principles espoused by Socrates. The Academy, considered the world's first university, would produce new generations of thinkers, notably Aristotle, Plato's greatest pupil. And perhaps most significant to the legacy of Socrates, Plato penned his dialogues, which would preserve Socrates's greatest contributions to critical thought and help damage the reputation of his critics.

But Socrates did not just influence philosophers. Even today, the impact of the Socratic method can be seen in college, graduate school, and even high school classes. Teachers and professors of nearly every subject often use the same process Socrates used to guide their students' thinking. In nearly every profession, concerns about ethical practices are ever-present. Business ethics, bioethics, legal ethics, and cyberethics are just some examples of applied ethics that can trace their origins to Socrates's ponderings on morality and virtue. And nearly everyone from any walk of life, when confronted with issues of moral, ethical, political, or cultural import in their daily lives, would stand to benefit by employing Socrates's fearless questioning and his reasoned and systematic approach to problems.

TIMELINE

499 BCE The Persian Empire attacks Greek city-states, and Athens sends troops to aid its Greek neighbors. The Persian Wars begin.

486 BCE The Persian army destroys the Athenian acropolis during its campaign to invade Athens.

479 BCE The Persian Wars end with Persia's defeat. Athens is the leading victor and rises to prominence.

CIRCA 479 BCE Athens forms the Delian League, a jointly funded military alliance, with other city-states as a protection against future Persian attacks.

CIRCA 470 BCE Socrates is born on Mount Lycabettus, located on the outskirts of Athens.

460 BCE Pericles becomes statesman-general and rises quickly in Athens's Assembly. This period marks the beginning of Athens's golden age, a time of relative peace, prosperity, creativity, and reconstruction.

447 BCE Phidias directs the building of the Parthenon, a project that showcases Athens's wealth and power. The monument serves as a tribute to Athens's patron goddess Athena, the goddess of wisdom and war.

CIRCA 440 BCE Chaerephon visits the oracle at Delphi, where Socrates is proclaimed the wisest man of all. The oracle's declaration launches Socrates's search to define wisdom, a quest that lasts throughout his life.

432 BCE Socrates serves as a hoplite in a battle against Potidaea, a Spartan ally, during which he forms a friendship with Alcibiades, who will later betray Athens and compromise Socrates's standing in Athenian society.

431 BCE The Peloponnesian War begins with Sparta and its allies pitted against Athens.

CIRCA 431 BCE An unknown plague infects Athens, claiming at least 25 percent of Athens's population. Pericles and his family die from the plague in 429 BCE.

CIRCA 428 BCE Plato, Socrates's most famous disciple, is born.

CIRCA 420 BCE Socrates marries Xanthippe. They eventually have three sons together.

404 BCE The Peloponnesian War ends in Athens's defeat, and Sparta replaces Athens's democratic government with the rule of the Thirty Tyrants. This marks the end of Athens's golden age.

399 BCE Meletus files charges against Socrates, accusing him of corrupting the youth and worshipping gods not sanctioned by the state. Socrates goes to trial, is found guilty, and is sentenced to die. Socrates drinks a cup of poisonous hemlock and dies in prison.

GLOSSARY

ACADEMY The school founded by Plato in 387 BCE, which is regarded as the world's first true university. The institution focused on instruction of philosophy and science and was shut down in 529 CE, more than nine hundred years after its establishment. Plato, a student of Socrates's, was partly inspired to open the school by his mentor's unjust death.

AGORA Marketplace. The agora served as the center of commerce and trade and as a meeting place for Athenians in ancient times. Socrates chose to engage in philosophical debates at the agora because it was the busiest spot in Athens and thus where his ideas would reach the greatest number of people.

COSMOLOGY The study of the universe, including its structure and origins.

DELIAN LEAGUE A military alliance founded around 479 BCE by Athens and hundreds of other Greek city-states for protection against future attacks from outsiders, especially Persians.

DIALECTIC A dialogue that includes examining, discussing, and reasoning through conflicting ideas as a way to discover truth.

ELENCHUS The logical refutation of an argument by proving the opposite of the argument's conclusion to be true.

ETHICS A branch of philosophy centered around questions of what is morally right and wrong, how these questions impact human behavior and society, and where moral responsibility lies.

GADFLY A person who provokes and annoys persistently. Socrates called himself the gadfly of Athens because of his constant badgering of passersby to engage him in philosophical debates.

GOLDEN AGE A time of peace, prosperity, and happiness. Athens's golden age was from around 460 BCE to the end of the fifth century BCE. During this era, Athens was ruled by a popular democracy, the city-state had ample funds to spend on projects to improve and beautify the city, and Athenians lived in relative peace and happiness. The period is regarded as one of the most progressive times in both Athenian and Greek history.

HOPLITE A Greek foot soldier who provided his own armor. During the fifth century BCE, hoplites were usually drawn from the middle classes because they could afford their own military gear.

MORALITY Beliefs about what constitutes right and wrong and the behaviors that fall in each category.

ORACLE A shrine built to honor a god in ancient Greece; a priest or priestess at the shrine through whom the honored god would speak; the message delivered by such a priest or priestess. The oracle at Delphi was the most visited of ancient Greece and the one who proclaimed Socrates as the wisest man.

PHILOSOPHY Literally meaning "love of wisdom" in Greek, philosophy is a discipline that centers around the inquiry into truth and morality and the creation of a system of ideas based on the results of such inquiries. Socrates is regarded as one of the early Western philosophers.

PIETY Respect for and obedience to one or more gods.

POLIS The Greek term for a city-state. In ancient Greece, there were more than a hundred poleis in the Mediterranean, each with its own separate government that was independent from the governments of other city-states.

SCAPEGOAT A person who is forced to bear the blame for other people's sins or for the wrongs of all of society.

SOCRATIC METHOD A method of philosophical inquiry devised by Socrates that uses a series of questions to expose the weaknesses of one's assumptions and replace them with beliefs that seem closer to the truth. Socrates would pose questions such as "What is truth?" and "What is virtue?" and ask question after question until his listeners could provide a reasonable, workable definition or answer. A major characteristic of the Socratic method is that it involves conversation and debate with at least one other person.

SOPHISTS Highly regarded teachers in ancient Greece who traveled throughout the city-states and taught philosophy and rhetoric to their disciples for a fee.

For More Information

The American Classical League (ACL)

860 NW Washington Boulevard, Suite A

Hamilton, OH 45013

(800) 670-8346

Website: http://www.aclclassics.org

The ACL supports the study of classical
languages throughout the United States and
Canada. It offers various scholarships and
teaching resources and sponsors workshop
tours of ancient Greek and Roman sites.

American Philosophical Society (APS)

104 South Fifth Street

Philadelphia, PA 19106

(215) 440-3400

Website: http://www.amphilsoc.org

APS supports research and discovery in the
humanities and sciences as well as scholars
in the fields of civic and cultural affairs. Its
extensive research library of manuscripts and
collections is available to scholars engaged in
various pursuits.

The Ancient Philosophy Society (APS)

Website: http://www.ancientphilosophysociety.org.

The APS brings together scholars of ancient Greek and Roman texts and philosophy for an annual meeting in order to encourage new interpretations of and critical engagement with ancient texts.

Association of Ancient Historians (AAH)

Website: http://associationofancienthistorians .org/index.html

The AAH brings together professionals engaged in the study of ancient history to present and discuss field research. The organization also sponsors meetings and shares updates and important information through its publications.

Canadian Philosophical Association (CPA)

P.O. Box 47077; rpo Blackburn Hamlet

Gloucester, ON K1B 5P9

Canada

Website: http://www.acpcpa.ca/en

The CPA organizes meetings and offers various

publications to support its goal of promoting the study of philosophy across Canada, both at the university level and before. It also supports professionals in the field and represents the field in public forums.

The Center for Ethics in Society

Stanford Law School

559 Nathan Abbott Way

Stanford, CA 94305

(650) 736-2629

Website: https://ethicsinsociety.stanford.edu

The Center for Ethics in Society works to shed light on various social issues—including extreme poverty, environmental sustainability, and international peace and security—by developing initiatives that bear an ethical dimension.

The Classical Association of Canada (CAC)

Department of Greek and Roman Studies

University of Victoria

Victoria, BC V8W 3P4

Canada

(250) 721-8528

Website: http://cac-scec.ca/wordpress

The CAC supports the study of ancient Greek and Roman civilizations and their significance in the modern world. It also promotes the teaching of classical languages in Canadian classrooms. Information on meetings, activities, scholarships, and more can be found on the CAC's website.

Socrates Café and Philosophers' Club

Website: http://www.philosopher.org/index.html

The Socrates Café and Philosophers' Club helps coordinate group gatherings in which individuals of all interests and backgrounds can come together to engage in Socratic dialogues on various philosophical inquiries.

University of Washington Center for Philosophy for Children

Box 353350

Department of Philosophy

University of Washington

Seattle, WA 98195

(206) 221-6297

Website: http://depts.washington.edu/nwcenter

The University of Washington's Center for Philosophy for Children encourages students in grades K–12 to explore philosophical questions and improve critical thinking through various classes, books, activities, and other resources. Teachers and parents can also find workshops that help them facilitate discussions of philosophy with K–12 students.

WEBSITES

Because of the changing nature of Internet links, Rosen Publishing has developed an online list of websites related to the subject of this book. This site is updated regularly. Please use this link to access the list:

http://www.rosenlinks.com/GGP/Soc

FOR FURTHER READING

Christian, James L. *Philosophy: An Introduction to the Art of Wondering*. Belmont, CA: Wadsworth, 2012.

Cohen, S. Marc, Patricia Curd, and C.D.C. Reeve, eds. *Readings in Ancient Greek Philosophy: From Thales to Aristotle*. Indianapolis, IN: Hackett Publishing, 2011.

Duignan, Brian, ed. *Ancient Philosophy: From 600 BCE to 500 CE*. New York, NY: Britannica Educational Publishing, 2011.

Duignan, Brian, ed. *Thinkers and Theories in Ethics*. New York, NY: Britannica Educational Publishing, 2011.

Hughes, Bettany. *The Hemlock Cup: Socrates, Athens and the Search for the Good Life*. New York, NY: Vintage, 2012.

Johnson, Paul. *Socrates: A Man for Our Times*. New York, NY: Penguin, 2011.

Jowett, Benjamin, trans. *The Trial and Death of Socrates: Four Dialogues*. New York, NY: Dover, 2010.

Kenny, Anthony. *A New History of Western Philosophy*. New York, NY: Oxford University Press, 2014.

Kleinman, Paul. *Philosophy 101: From Plato and Socrates to Ethics and Metaphysics, An Essential*

Primer on the History of Thought. Avon, MA: F+W Media, 2013.

Kreeft, Peter. *Philosophy 101 by Socrates: An Introduction to Philosophy via Plato's Apology*. South Bend, IN: St. Augustine's Press, 2012.

Kreeft, Peter. *Socrates' Children: Ancient*. South Bend, IN: St. Augustine's Press, 2015.

Kreeft, Peter. *Socratic Logic: A Logic Text Using Socratic Method, Platonic Questions, and Aristotelian Principles*. South Bend, IN: St. Augustine's Press, 2010.

Melchert, Norman. *The Great Conversation: A Historical Introduction to Philosophy*. New York, NY: Oxford University Press, 2014.

Miller, James. *Examined Lives: From Socrates to Nietzsche*. New York, NY: Farrar, Strauss and Giroux, 2011.

Nagle, Jeanne, ed. *Top 101 Philosophers*. New York, NY: Britannica Educational Publishing, 2014.

Rudebusch, George. *Socrates*. Malden, MA: Wiley, 2009.

Shields, Christopher. *Ancient Philosophy: A Contemporary Introduction*. New York, NY: Routledge, 2012.

Smith, Robert Rowland. *Breakfast with Socrates: An Extraordinary (Philosophical) Journey Through Your Day*. New York, NY: Free Press, 2009.

Solomon, Robert C., and Kathleen M. Higgins. *The Big Questions: A Short Introduction to Philosophy.* Belmont, CA: Wadsworth, 2010.

Strathern, Paul. *Socrates: Philosophy in an Hour.* New York, NY: HarperCollins, 2013.

Waterfield, Robin. *Why Socrates Died: Dispelling the Myths.* New York, NY: W.W. Norton, 2009.

BIBLIOGRAPHY

Ancient-Greece.org. "Temple of Apollo at Delphi." Retrieved December 12, 2014 (http://ancient-greece.org/architecture/delphi-temple-of-apollo.html).

Britannica School. "Delphi." Retrieved December 10, 2014 (http://school.eb.com/levels/middle/article/273959).

Connolly, Tim. "Plato: Phaedo." Internet Encyclopedia of Philosophy. Retrieved December 9, 2014 (http://www.iep.utm.edu/phaedo).

Encyclopædia Britannica Online. "Socrates." Retrieved December 9, 2014 (http://original.search.eb.com/eb/article-233638).

History.com. "Socrates." Retrieved December 5, 2014 (http://www.history.com/topics/ancient-history/socrates).

Internet Sacred Text Archive. "Dialogues of Plato." Retrieved December 4, 2014 (http://www.sacred-texts.com/cla/plato).

Linder, Doug. "The Trial of Socrates." 2002. Retrieved December 10, 2014 (http://law2.umkc.edu/faculty/projects/ftrials/socrates/socratesaccount.html).

Magee, Bryan. *The Story of Philosophy*. New York, NY: DK Publishing, Inc., 2001.

Maxwell, Max. "Introduction to the Socratic Method and Its Effect on Critical Thinking." Retrieved December 9, 2014 (http://www.socraticmethod.net).

Nails, Debra. "Socrates." Stanford Encyclopedia of Philosophy, March 19, 2014. Retrieved December 12, 2014 (http://plato.stanford.edu/entries/socrates).

Nardo, Don. *The Trial of Socrates*. San Diego, CA: Lucent Books, Inc., 1997.

Plato. *The Republic and Other Works*. New York, NY: Doubleday, 1989.

20-20 Site. "Socrates: A Biography of Socrates' Life." 2002. Retrieved December 10, 2014 (http://www.2020site.org/socrates).

Winter, Laurie. "Born to Check Mail." *New York Times*, July 16, 2010. Retrieved November 30, 2014 (http://www.nytimes.com/2010/07/18/books/review/Winer-t.html?_r=3&ref=-books&).

INDEX

ABOUT THE AUTHORS

Natasha Dhillon is a writer and classics enthusiast from Washington, D.C. She majored in philosophy in college where she first learned about Socrates and had the opportunity to engage with fellow students and professors using the Socratic method. She can often be found exploring the antiquities and art housed in the capital city's museums.

Jun Lim first learned about the Socratic method of questioning in college. Jun, like Socrates, believes that individuals can make significant contributions to society only after answering self-directed questions designed to examine one's own ethical and moral beliefs, and that each person carries a personal responsibility in the effort to create an ethical world. Jun was raised in Oregon.

PHOTO CREDITS